THE
ONE-MINUTE
SELF✸CARE
JOURNAL

365 Ways to Nurture Your
Physical, Mental, and Emotional
Well-Being Every Day

EVA OLSEN

CASTLE POINT BOOKS
NEW YORK

THE ONE-MINUTE SELF-CARE JOURNAL.
Copyright © 2022 by St. Martin's Press.
All rights reserved. Printed in Malaysia.
For information, address St. Martin's Publishing Group,
120 Broadway, New York, NY 10271.

www.castlepointbooks.com

The Castle Point Books trademark is owned by
Castle Point Publishing, LLC.
Castle Point books are published and distributed by
St. Martin's Publishing Group.

ISBN 978-1-250-28171-5 (trade paperback)

Design by Noora Cox
Images used under license by Shutterstock.com

Our books may be purchased in bulk for promotional,
educational, or business use.

Please contact your local bookseller or the Macmillan
Corporate and Premium Sales Department at
1-800-221-7945, extension 5442, or by email at
MacmillanSpecialMarkets@macmillan.com.

First Edition: 2022

Printed in Malaysia

10 9 8 7 6 5 4 3 2 1

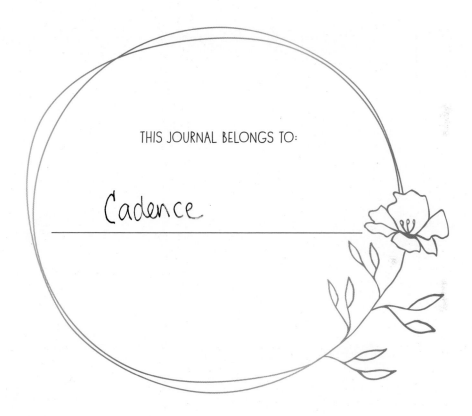

THIS JOURNAL BELONGS TO:

Cadence

We turn not older with years
but newer every day.

—EMILY DICKINSON

WE ALL WANT TO BE AT OUR BEST—PHYSICALLY, MENTALLY, AND EMOTIONALLY. But how do we find the time? The smart path: Take one little step of self-care each day and let all the good build up, with the help of this book. Get ready to be surprised and feel loved through hundreds of self-care options that surround you!

The 365 prompts on the pages that follow are designed to be simple ways of bringing out your beauty and strength. By focusing inward for just a minute or two, you can feel more present and able to tackle whatever life throws at you. With *The One-Minute Self-Care Journal*, treating yourself with extra kindness will become your new superpower!

1. WRAP YOURSELF IN WARMTH—pull a cozy blanket around you, put on a favorite flannel shirt or cardigan, or ask for a hug from a loved one. How does the physical warmth make you feel emotionally? When can you regularly turn to this simple act of self-care?

Warmth from favorite sweat pants, cozy blanket, and of course, Flynn. Physical warmth makes me feel safe and less alone. I can find ways to seek warmth at home (hot shower, quick nap) or elsewhere (oversized sweater, heating pad @ office)

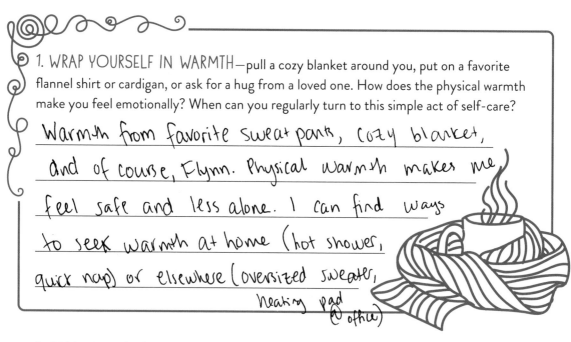

2. READ ONE PAGE of something you love—whether it's a book of poetry, an old letter, or a beach read. What words or thoughts stand out?

_____

_____

_____

_____

BONUS: Keep reading longer if you like!

3. WASH YOUR HANDS under warm water. As you wash, gently massaging your hands, what regrets or stresses can you release down the drain?

_____   _____

_____   _____

_____   _____

4. LIST FIVE CHARACTER TRAITS (strength, patience, determination, compassion. . .) you need to get through this week. Then step outside, take a deep breath, and imagine you're drawing in just what you need.

1. _____

2. _____

3. _____

4. _____

5. _____

5. BUY YOURSELF A SMALL GIFT. Have it wrapped luxuriously, as you would a present for a good friend, then put it in a place where you will see it and anticipate unwrapping it . . . tomorrow. Sketch the pretty package here.

6. GO AHEAD, UNWRAP THAT GIFT. What did you choose and what does it mean to you?

_____

_____

_____

_____

7. KICK OFF YOUR SHOES

and "root" your bare feet into the ground—whether you're near soft grass, warm sand, or shaggy carpet. Standing with your feet parallel, grip the ground firmly as if you have roots growing from your feet. Fill the space at right with words that describe how rooting makes you feel.

8. DEDICATE A SONG TO YOURSELF. What lyrics capture something you need to hear right now? Write them below, then carry the words in your head throughout the day.

_____

_____

_____

9. PLANT SOMETHING. Toss wildflower seeds into an open space. Add herbs to a kitchen windowsill. Bring home a colorful container of blooms to display in an outdoor area. Draw the beautiful results you're enjoying now or awaiting. No green thumb? In the space below, plant the seed of an idea you've been carrying around.

TO DO

10. GIVE YOURSELF AN EXTENSION. What's one thing on your to-do list for this week that can honestly wait in order to grant yourself some breathing space?

11. CREATE A PICK-ME-UP NOTE OR CARD to remind yourself of how strong you are. Jot a few words of encouragement from it below.

_____

_____

_____

BONUS: Seal it in an envelope addressed to yourself, then ask a trusted person in your life to mail it when they sense you're going through a tough time.

12. TAKE A BEAUTIFUL PHOTO—a selfie, or a picture of a beloved person or pet, an outdoor view, your favorite coffee mug filled to the brim—for your eyes only. No posting to social, just post it here.

13. OUTLINE A MORNING ROUTINE. Include at least one simple thing that will start the day on a beautiful note. It can be as simple as giving yourself a hug, stretching before your feet hit the floor, taking a minute to look outside, or breathing in deeply three times.

_____

_____

_____

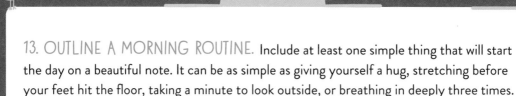

14. LIGHT A CANDLE. As you light the wick, think about where _you_ want to spark this week. Promise yourself what you need to shine brightly.

I WANT TO SHINE IN THIS SPACE: _____ .

I WILL GIVE MYSELF _____ , _____ ,

AND _____ TO MAKE THAT HAPPEN.

15. SET A BUDGET FOR SELF-CARE. Put your money where your focus is! What can you afford on a weekly or monthly basis to solely feed your spirit?

_____   _____

_____   _____

_____   _____

BONUS: Designate a way to set that money aside—a special jar, pretty envelope, or dedicated savings account.

16. SEE THE VALUE. What do you appreciate about your job?

_____

_____

_____

17. KNOW YOUR NONNEGOTIABLES. What is unacceptable in your relationships? Remind yourself of what you deserve.

_____

_____

_____

18. MAKE A SIGNATURE MUG.

Choose a basic hot beverage to enjoy. Then add something a little extra—ginger, dark chocolate chips, fresh mint leaves, a cinnamon stick, whatever jazzes it up for you. Give your drink a fancy menu name that describes how you want it to make you feel, and believe in the effect as you sip. Incredibly Calming Cinnamon Chai, anyone?

DRINK SPECIAL

_____

_____

_____

_____

19. SIGN UP. Register for an online course—anything from an ongoing fun fitness class to a onetime wine-tasting session. Don't worry about practical outcomes or applications! What do you choose?

_____

_____

_____

20. HEAD TO BED EARLY. Even if you don't go to sleep right away, give yourself time and space to rest. What's in, on, or near your bed to make it the most relaxing experience for you?

IN: _____

ON: _____

NEAR: _____

21. SAY YES. Be ready to say yes to something today that feels right in your heart—even if your head attempts to overthink it. Color in the word yes as your intention below.

22. SHOUT A WORD OF RELEASE. It can be a swear word or just a very strong word (real or even made up) that releases any frustration you're feeling. Find a place where you can shout without turning any heads. What word did you choose? How did it feel?

23. SET A PJ DATE. Make an appointment on your calendar and here for a stay-in-your-pajamas day.

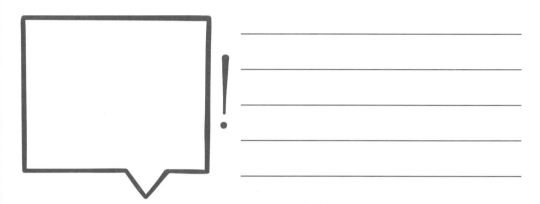

24. TRY TAPPING. Emotional freedom technique (EFT), also known as tapping, focuses on working energy points on the body with your fingertips to release difficult or stuck feelings. To give it a try, choose a point to tap, then fill in the blank with an affirmation you can use while you tap.

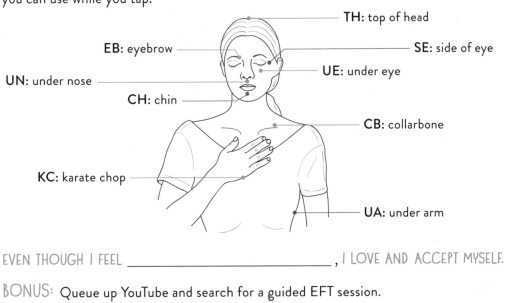

EB: eyebrow

UN: under nose

CH: chin

KC: karate chop

TH: top of head

SE: side of eye

UE: under eye

CB: collarbone

UA: under arm

EVEN THOUGH I FEEL _____ , I LOVE AND ACCEPT MYSELF.

BONUS: Queue up YouTube and search for a guided EFT session.

25. ASK FOR HELP. Drop the guilt and ask for what you need! What simple call, email, or text will take one thing off your to-do list or get you support to make it easier?

_____

_____

_____

26. CREATE A PLAYLIST. Your list should be filled with songs that make you feel as wonderful and strong as you are.

_____   _____

_____   _____

_____   _____

_____   _____

_____

27. DREAM UP AN EVENING ROUTINE. What will settle you into peaceful sleep? It can be as simple as laying out clothing for the next day, washing your face, or granting yourself screen-free time. Then start tonight!

_____

_____

_____

28. RUB IT IN. Sum up what you need most today in one word (energy, forgiveness, support, soothing...), then write it in the space at right. As you say the word to yourself, rub a bit of moisturizer into any part of your body—from your temples to your feet.

29. DRESS FOR AN OCCASION. Choose an outfit, then let it lead you someplace fun. Where do you go?

_____

_____

_____

30. STRETCH YOUR COMFORT. Where can you do a little extra today in a healthy way? Do one more burpee? Talk with one new contact? Hold your tongue for one more minute before responding?

_____

_____

_____

31. PICTURE CALM. Place a calming photo somewhere you tend to feel high levels of stress—on your desk, inside your checkbook, in your car. Describe the photo and the space where you've placed it.

_____

_____

_____

_____

32. SILENCE YOUR SOCIAL MEDIA. Put up a brief note stating that you're taking the day off from social media but will welcome direct contacts. Then follow through. How do you feel at the end of the day?

_____

_____

_____

_____

33. LAUGH OUT LOUD. What is guaranteed to make you laugh? Record it below as a reminder whenever you need it, then do it!

_____

_____

_____

34. ENJOY A SMOOTHIE. As your drink comes together—whether you order it or make it yourself—think about what ingredients in your life (no matter how diverse or unexpected) are blending perfectly right now. List them below with gratitude.

_____ ♥ _____ ♥ _____

_____ ♥ _____

35. MAKE YOUR BED. As you pull up the covers, think about what you want to tuck into your day—maybe calm, adventure, or companionship. Record those priorities below.

_____

_____

_____

_____

36. TAKE A GRATITUDE WALK. Wherever you are, take some steps and record anything pleasant you experience—from what you see (faces of familiar people or majestic trees) to what you hear (people laughing or birds singing).

_____

_____

_____

_____

_____

37. LOCATE YOUR QUIET. For times when you just need a little silence, list a few places you can go—within your home and within your town.

_____   _____

_____   _____

_____   _____

_____   _____

38. COLOR YOUR WORLD. How can you add more of a color to your day that makes you feel fab—in your wardrobe or as a feature of a bath bomb? Choose your color burst below.

39. START A VISION BOARD. Whether you choose to create a physical or an online version, make some notes here about what you want to include. Think about what inspires you and what you want to manifest in your life.

40. REACH OUT. Who do you need to connect with today to put a smile on your face? Don't make excuses about it not being a convenient time. Connect in person, by phone, or by text—all it takes is a minute to feel like everything is right in the world.

_____

_____

_____

41. CELEBRATE THIS DAY. What good things in your life do you keep saving for some special day or special someone—the champagne glasses, those sequins? Break them out today to remind yourself that you are special and this day is special! Post a pic below.

42. CREATE A SANCTUARY. What's one thing you can easily add to your bathroom to make it a more relaxing space—softer towels, a plant, a calming candle? Sketch it here, then make it happen in real life.

43. FIND MOVEMENT. It's easy to feel stuck from time to time. Where can you go to get inspired by movement in just minutes—a river or ocean, a zoo, or even a racetrack? Make a plan for where and when you'll go in the next few days. Nothing nearby? Try a virtual visit.

_____

_____

_____

_____

_____

44. PACK YOUR NEEDS. Before you head out for the day, make a list of what to bring along to be prepared with comfort and care.

_____   _____

_____   _____

_____   _____

45. TURN OFF THE NEWS. One day won't take you completely out of touch. How do you feel when you take a break? How can you set boundaries around media every day?

_____

_____

_____

46. MAKE THAT APPOINTMENT. What appointment have you been putting off but need to make in order to take care of yourself—a general physical, a dental cleaning, an eye exam, even a snip of those split ends? Draw a smiley-faced you next to the date of the appointment.

47. CHANGE YOUR SCENERY. Rearrange a few items in your house. Try a new route to work or a regular errand stop. Or try a different coffee shop. Post or draw a pic of the newness you experience.

48. ROLL AWAY STRESS. Place a tennis ball or other small ball under your bare foot. What stressful parts of your day do you feel fading away as you press down into the ball and roll it around?

_____

_____

_____

_____

49. TREAT YOURSELF TO ART. Whether you purchase it or create it yourself, give yourself the gift of artwork that inspires you. What do you choose? Where will you place it for maximum impact?

_____

_____

_____

_____

_____

50. FOCUS. Drop the frenzy! Whatever you do today, try to take it one task at a time. Immerse yourself in making dinner—don't try to sort the mail and answer emails at the same time. How does it feel?

_____

_____

_____

_____

_____

51. START FRESH. Come up with a morning message of self-love and hope that you can say each day as your feet hit the floor. (Example: "Today is a new day full of gifts for me.") Write it in lively letters below.

52. STRETCH. With your feet rooted in the ground, stretch your interlaced hands overhead. Feel yourself reach just a little farther. Bring your arms slightly to one side, hold; return to center and move to the other side to hold a stretch. Make a note about where you could stretch yourself just a bit more to reach goals in your life today.

_____

_____

_____

_____

53. BE A POSER. Try a yoga power pose—Goddess and Warrior are fierce. (It's easy to find how-tos online.) Record how it makes you feel.

_____

_____

_____

54. ASK AN EXPERT. Release yourself from the expectation that you should magically know it all. Who in your world holds answers that could be helpful in your life? Allow yourself to be vulnerable and ask for guidance or information.

_____

_____

_____

55. BUY YOURSELF A BOOK. Don't let it sit in the store window or in your online cart! In your hands? Read at least a few pages and record below some words that stuck with you. Awaiting delivery? Sketch the cover below as you eagerly anticipate diving into the words inside.

AM PM

56. SET A DAILY REMINDER. Use the tools on your phone to remind yourself to simply rest and breathe deeply at least once a day. At what time of day do you need this designated break the most?

57. FEEL THE WIND. Find a way to enjoy the rush of wind through your hair—ride a bike, walk at a quick pace, drive with the windows down, or even turn on a fan and get silly with a selfie photo shoot. How does it feel?

_____

_____

_____

_____

58. MOVE OUTSIDE. What parts of your day can you move outside, or at least near a window, when the weather cooperates—enjoying a morning cup of coffee, eating lunch, opening mail? Make a list of ideas to choose from anytime you need to brighten your outlook.

_____   _____

_____   _____

_____   _____

_____   _____

_____

59. BE PERFECTLY IMPERFECT. The dishwasher will work just fine even if you don't arrange its contents perfectly. How can you ease a ton of stress by doing something good enough today?

_____

_____

_____

_____

60. SPEAK UP. What words have you been holding back that would be freeing for you to say today? Write them here and then speak them at the right time.

61. SWITCH UP DINNER. If you usually eat alone, invite a special guest to dine with you one night this week. If you usually eat with an entourage, set aside one relaxed meal alone. What's your plan?

_____

_____

_____

62. KEEP HEALTHY CONTACT. Define how you want to stay in touch with loved ones. How often is enough? How much is too much? What ways feel best? Think about the balance between closeness and the space you need, then work out shared expectations.

_____

_____

_____

63. START A NEW SAVINGS PLAN. What is something you've always wanted to do just for you but couldn't justify the expense? Start a special savings fund to make that dream a reality.

_____

_____

_____

64. CLEAR THE HURDLE. Think about the toughest thing on your agenda today. Promise yourself here to knock it out early and enjoy the rest of your day!

_____

_____

_____

65. EXAMINE YOUR ESCAPES. When you're having a tough day, what little escapes do you use that are healthy? Do you turn to any escapes that aren't good for you in the long run?

HEALTHY   NOT SO GOOD

_____   _____

_____   _____

_____   _____

66. FOLLOW THROUGH WITH "UNFOLLOW." What social media accounts on your feed bring up feelings that don't feed self-care and healthy growth? Don't let them bring you down any longer!

_____   _____

_____   _____

_____   _____

67. KNOW YOUR WORTH. Make a list of what you love about yourself. You can start with your self-care efforts!

_____   _____

_____   _____

_____   _____

_____   _____

68. STEP INTO ACTION. What do you need most today? Circle your choice below and commit to the action. Or come up with another idea that fits what you need.

» ADVENTURE OR DISCOVERY: *Visit someplace you've never been and walk around.*

» COMFORT OR SECURITY: *Place a cozy pair of slippers or socks by the door to slip into as soon as you come home.*

» FRESH START: *Immerse your feet in a bath and feel the weight of the day wash away.*

» _____ : _____

69. FLIP THE SCRIPT. What negative messages or doubts went through your head in the past few days? How can you turn those words in a more positive direction? Self-talk matters!

NEGATIVE   ⟶   POSITIVE

_____   _____

_____   _____

_____   _____

_____   _____

70. CELEBRATE YOU. Self-care can be simply recognizing your efforts. What are you most proud of in your life right now?

_____

_____

_____

71. LISTEN TO YOUR BODY. What does your body need today? Pay attention to the messages it sends, as you would a good friend, and do your best to respond.

_____

_____

_____

72. FIX IT FAST. Replace those batteries or sew on that button. What little task has been on your to-do list for a while that you can complete right now? Write it below with a big check mark next to it. You'll get satisfaction from one fewer thing left undone.

☐ _____

☐ _____

☐ _____

☐ _____

73. FORGIVE LIKE A FRIEND. Whatever disappointment you're holding on to, write yourself a message of forgiveness or acceptance. Speak to yourself as you would to a good friend.

_____

_____

_____

74. CHECK YOUR SOLES. If any of your shoes look great from the top but questionable on the bottom, it's time to let them go—no matter how much you've grown attached. Make a list of any categories that need replacements—for example, black dress shoes or cross-trainers.

_____   _____

_____   _____

_____   _____

75. BUY YOURSELF A BOUQUET. What word comes to mind for how the flowers make you feel? Write it below and return to the word and feeling throughout the day.

76. STARGAZE. Taking in a twinkling sky can put everything in perspective and make us feel connected to something greater. Look up and draw what the sky shows you below.

77. PAMPER YOUR SMILE. Devote a little extra time to your teeth today. Then post a photo of yourself smiling big below.

BONUS: If anything is holding you back from sharing your smile regularly, schedule an appointment with a dentist to talk through options.

78. THANK YOUR SUPPORT. Who or what can you always depend on? Fill in the blank below.

THANK YOU, _____.

79. CARRY A STONE. Whether your stone is a beach find or a store-bought crystal, assign it a word with a quality you need—maybe *strength* or *calm*. Then carry the stone with you throughout the day. Whenever you feel things begin to spin out of control, rub your stone's surface and say the word to bring you back to something solid. Draw your stone with the word inside it at right.

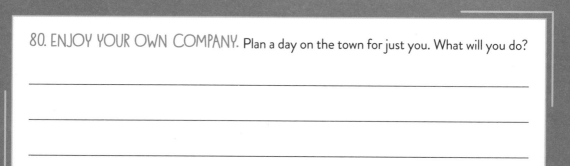

80. ENJOY YOUR OWN COMPANY. Plan a day on the town for just you. What will you do?

_____

_____

_____

81. BREAK OUT THE CRAYONS or colored pens or pencils. Find a fun way to use them today—whether it's in a coloring book or simply taking colorful meeting notes. How did color bring you joy?

_____

_____

_____

82. TOY AROUND. Treat yourself to something a little silly—maybe play dough, bubbles, or a punching balloon. Then lose the cares of the day in play. Draw yourself being a big kid below.

83. GET INSPIRED. Look around your space. What inspires you to take some sort of action? Sneakers begging for a run or walk? Colored pens pushing you to be creative? Phone sitting near you, hinting that you should make a call? Go with your gut and what grabs your attention.

_____

_____

_____

84. RATE YOUR DAY. Rate how well you treated yourself today. What went well? What could have been better?

☺   😐   ☹   >:<   😮

_____

_____

_____

85. ADD AN APP. What wellness apps could contribute to your self-care? Make a list and star at least one you'll try this week.

_____   _____

_____   _____

_____   _____

86. MOVE WITH JOY. Make a list of ways you can give your body the gift of movement throughout the day.

_____   _____

_____   _____

_____   _____

_____   _____

87. WATCH THE TIME. What hour of the day tends to fill you with the most dread? Is there anything you can change about the circumstances? Can you sandwich the time with more calm and joy?

_____

_____

_____

_____

_____

88. GO THERE. What place is powerfully calming to you? It could be a coffee shop around the corner or an island getaway. If you can't go there in person today, find an online or personal video that brings the ambience to you.

BONUS: Post a pic of the place or screenshot of the video above.

89. FEEL CONNECTED.
What are your strongest connections—both interpersonal and within the community or larger world? Are there more connections waiting to be made?

90. MAKE IT FOR YOU. Choose a favorite meal you'll treat yourself to this week—whether you enjoy cooking it or will be ordering it from a restaurant. What's on the menu?

91. TAME THAT TENSION. What part of your body feels most tense? How can you show it some care—a hot shower, gentle rubbing?

_____

_____

_____

92. GO A LITTLE LUX. What simple luxury can you give yourself today? Do it!

_____

_____

_____

93. LISTEN TO PRAISE. What positive words would your family and friends use to describe you? List them below and believe them.

_____   _____

_____   _____

_____   _____

94. KNOW YOUR VALUES. From the list of positive words you wrote above, choose two or three qualities that are most important to you. Whenever you feel overwhelmed, bring your focus back to what's important to live by your values.

_____   _____   _____

95. LINK WITH A WISH BUDDY. Who in your life can you exchange good wishes with each morning? Agree to share a word of in-person encouragement or send a short text or email to start each other's day off on a positive note. Record your first exchange below and note how it feels to have that simple but steady support.

_____

_____

_____

_____

96. BUBBLE-BREATHE. Inhale slowly through your nose for four seconds, hold for two seconds, then exhale through pursed lips for four seconds, as if you were blowing bubbles that are carrying your stress far way. Wait two seconds, then repeat. Fill in the bubbles below with the stressful situations you are releasing.

97. SYNC WITH THE SUN. Choose a day to watch the sunrise or sunset. Capture the experience in words or a drawing or a photo below.

98. ENJOY GOOD-MOOD FOOD. What food makes you feel amazing as you're savoring it and after as well—maybe a fresh, juicy orange or a bite of dark chocolate? How can you enjoy it today and a few more times this week?

_____

_____

_____

99. GET GROUNDED. When your world seems to be spinning out of control, list three paths to feeling grounded again (talking to a certain person, taking deep breaths or a long walk). Try one now if you need it.

1. _____

2. _____

3. _____

100. SEEK WEIRD AND WILD. What is something you've been holding back from doing because others might consider it a little (or a lot) crazy? Take a step into the weird or wild today!

_____

_____

_____

101. FEEL THAT PHOTO. Choose a special photo to place on your nightstand. Take a minute to focus on it before you go to sleep and when you first wake up. Describe the photo or post a copy of it below.

102. GIVE THANKS FOR THE MIX. Just as healthy foods feed the body, healthy relationships feed the spirit. What are the ingredients of a healthy relationship in your life that make it work?

_____   _____

_____   _____

_____   _____

_____   _____

103. PROMISE YOURSELF BETTER. In what recent situations could you have treated yourself better? Give yourself a do-over in the second column. How will you treat yourself with more kindness and grace going forward?

_____   _____

_____   _____

_____   _____

_____   _____

104. RECLAIM DOWNTIME. When do you wish you had "unplugged" in the past week? How can you avoid tech temptation next time?

_____

_____

_____

_____

105. LIST YOUR WEEK. What do you feel you need to accomplish this week? It can feel good to get everything down on paper and off your mind.

_____   _____

_____   _____

_____   _____

_____   _____

106. LOWER THE PRESSURE. Go back and take a look at the list you created above. Cross off at least three to-do tasks that honestly don't need to be done—at least, this week. How does it feel to give yourself some breathing room?

_____

_____

_____

_____

_____

107. ACKNOWLEDGE YOUR FEELINGS. How are you truly feeling today?

Give yourself space to be honest with those feelings. If you're sad, let the tears out. If you're happy, jump up and down. If you're angry, punch a pillow. How can you healthfully express your feelings right now?

_____

_____

_____

_____

_____

108. DO A HAPPY DANCE. Think of something you can celebrate today. What inspires your happy dance and what's your theme song?

_____

_____

_____

_____

109. GIVE YOURSELF MORE. What do you need more of in your life—travel, time alone or with others, good food, adventure? Tell yourself you deserve it and create a plan to make it happen!

_____

_____

_____

_____

110. TAKE A BREAK. What is normally part of your day that it would feel good to take a rest from? Grant yourself the break you need.

_____

_____

_____

111. CHANNEL YOUR INNER CHILD. Do something that makes you feel like a kid—maybe dipping cookies in milk, coloring, or watching cartoons. What do you choose?

_____

_____

_____

112. HOLD THE LINE. What are some things you're proud to say you've never done? Salute staying true to yourself and what's good for your mental and physical health.

_____

_____

_____

113. SEE THE ACCOMPLISHMENTS. What are some things you accomplished today? Even if it was a seemingly unproductive day, getting out of bed counts.

_____

_____

_____

_____

114. TRACK OVER TIME. What have you accomplished in the past year? Celebrate the power of time.

_____

_____

_____

_____

115. CARRY A KEY. What unlocks the most opportunities for you—your persistence, patience, positivity . . . ? Write the quality on the key below and on an old key that you can carry with you for inspiration.

116. CHOOSE YOUR VIEW. Focus on something beautiful in your current surroundings. Sketch it.

117. WATCH THE WEATHER. Draw the silver lining in your last storm cloud.

118. SPLURGE ON SLEEP. Treat yourself by purchasing new sheets, pillows, PJs, or even a mattress. What do you splurge on? Post a pic or describe it.

119. ADD COMFORT. Look around your work space. What little touches could you add to make it more ergonomic and comfortable?

_____

_____

_____

_____

120. SHARE A SMILE. Lend a smile or good word to someone new who pops into your life. What was the reaction? How did it make you feel?

_____

_____

_____

121. MAKE A FINANCIAL MOVE. What's one simple step you can take to care for your finances? It could be anything from rounding up loose change for deposit to purchasing that stock you've been considering.

_____

_____

_____

122. PLAY THE GAME. What electronic game relaxes you—a word game, a home decorating app, a shape-sorting challenge? Treat yourself to one or two rounds, then note when playing it could help you relax—maybe before a doctor appointment or a stressful meeting.

_____

_____

_____

123. DRINK IT IN. What are you thirsty for more of in your life? As you sip a drink of your choice, promise yourself to follow through on finding ways to quench that thirst.

_____

_____

_____

124. APPRECIATE LIFE'S LESSONS. What's one little thing you learned recently that amazed you? How does it inspire you to keep learning?

_____

_____

_____

_____

125. BREATHE BY THE BOX. Trace each line of the box below, following the arrows and instructions.

START ❶ SIT UP STRAIGHT, SHOULDERS BACK.

FINISH

❷ BREATHE IN SLOWLY THROUGH YOUR NOSE.

❹ BREATHE OUT SLOWLY THROUGH YOUR MOUTH.

❸ HOLD YOUR BREATH FOR A COUNT OF FOUR.

BONUS: Practice tracing an imaginary square with your finger or in your mind so you can do a few box breaths anytime you need to calm down.

126. TAKE A MENTAL HEALTH DAY. Mark it on the calendar now and consider how you'll spend it.

_____

_____

_____

127. TOSS A WISH. You're never too old to toss a coin in a fountain and make a wish. No fountain in your travels today? Toss a stone into any body of water. What's your wish?

_____

_____

_____

_____

_____

128. MOVE ON. What knee-jerk response did you want to say or post today? Release it here.

_____

_____

_____

_____

_____

129. TRY FILM THERAPY. Think of a movie scene that matches your mood. Describe it or draw it here.

BONUS: Watch the scene or the entire movie.

130. SEEK A THRILL. What is one adventure you've always wanted to make happen? How can you take one step this week toward making it a reality?

_____

_____

_____

_____

131. BELIEVE. What people, experiences, or places make you believe in magic? How can you fill this week with more magic?

_____

_____

_____

132. STRETCH YOURSELF. Find a way to stretch your body, mind, or comfort zone today. How does it feel before and after you take the stretch?

_____

_____

_____

133. SING OUT LOUD. What song matches your current mood or is what you need to hear right now? Belt it out and jot down a few words of lyrical inspiration here.

BONUS: Set the song as your alarm or an alert.

134. APPRECIATE THE MISSES. What are some things you thankfully avoided today—whether you made good choices or the universe had your back?

_____

_____

_____

_____

_____

135. LOOK FOR BEAUTY. What's the most beautiful thing you saw this week? Sketch it or describe it.

136. LOVE YOUR SELFIE. Take a selfie that highlights your best feature. Post it here.

137. HAVE FUN WITH A FILTER. Take a selfie with a filter. Why did you choose that particular filter? What can it remind you in your everyday life?

_____

_____

_____

_____

138. SHOW GRATITUDE FOR CREATIVITY. Recount the best parts of your day in a creative way—a haiku, song lyrics, a comic strip or meme.

139. SURROUND WITH HAPPINESS. Who gives off the happiest vibes in your life? Set up time to spend with that person.

_____

_____

_____

140. TAKE A HARD PASS. What did you say no to this week that felt great?

_____

_____

_____

141. START A HEALTHY HABIT. No more "working up to it"! Whether it's boosting fruit and veggie intake or getting more steps in your day, start today—even in little bits. What action will you take?

_____

_____

_____

142. ACCEPT A MISTAKE. What's something you can now admit that you got totally wrong—and it's OK? Forgive yourself here and now.

_____

_____

_____

143. PLAN A PICNIC. Make one of your meals a picnic today. List the menu and any special accessories here. Cold or rainy? Take your picnic inside.

_____

_____

_____

_____

144. BUY A TICKET. Flight, concert, game, or charity event? Whatever you choose, record the details or a copy of the ticket below.

145. SORT YOUR THOUGHTS. Pay attention to everything positive going through your mind right now by writing those thoughts here in bright colors.

146. NIX THE NUMBERS. What numbers are becoming an obsession in your life—salary earnings, numbers on the scale or a waistband, social followers? Write the numbers, then top them with a big, bold *X*.

147. BOOK THE SPA. Make an appointment for a spa treatment. What's your splurge?

_____

_____

_____

_____

148. REVISIT A HAPPY TIME. Recall a special memory below.

_____

_____

_____

_____

_____

BONUS: Let others who are part of the memory know you were thinking of them and that special time.

149. SWEETEN THE DAY. What treat can add a little sweetness to your day—gourmet dark chocolate, fruit fresh from a farmers' market, coffee with a shot of special flavor?

_____

_____

_____

_____

_____

BONUS: Share the sweetness with a friend.

150. PLAN AN UPGRADE. What in your closet is long overdue for an upgrade? Hint: Check jackets, belts, and sneakers. List qualities to look for in your new purchase.

_____

_____

_____

151. ASK FOR WHAT YOU NEED. Reach out to a loved one and ask them to lend you their ear—whether you're looking for advice, inspiration, or comfort. When will you speak, and what do you need most?

_____

_____

_____

152. DROP IT. What do you need to drop—a grudge that's eating at you, an overcommitment that's weighing on you? Whatever it is, drop it here and move on.

153. BRING IN THE BLOOM. What flower or plant inspires you? How can you make it part of your surroundings—whether with a live plant, a print or photo, or even a scent?

_____

_____

_____

_____

154. COLLECT MEMORIES. Pick out a pretty journal or notebook to place on your coffee table and designate as a guest book. Friends and family can enjoy adding details of get-togethers and you can enjoy reading the memories anytime. Post a picture of the book along with a note about the first time you anticipate guests using it.

155. STRIKE A POSE. Taking a strong physical stance can make you feel more confident instantly. Describe or post a picture of a power pose that will work for you.

156. GIVE AND TAKE COMPLIMENTS. No excuses! Accept with a thank-you and give when you feel the nudge. How does it feel? Which compliments stand out to you?

_____

_____

_____

_____

157. FIND INNER WISDOM. Where are you interested in looking for more insight into who you are? List any tools you would consider—astrology, tarot cards, personality typing systems like the enneagram. Note one you can pursue this week.

_____

_____

_____

158. WAKE UP YOUR WATER. List a few ways you can make drinking more water easier or more delicious—like adding fresh fruit, drinking out of a pretty glass, setting a phone reminder. Then go get a glass!

_____

_____

_____

_____

159. START THE REEL. What movie title (real or sprung from your mind) captures the week you want to have? What will make it come to life?

_____

_____

_____

160. ENJOY LOCAL. What fresh food is grown in your area? What regional delights is your town known for? Treat yourself to a local favorite.

_____

_____

_____

161. TRY TRADITION ANYTIME. What is one family tradition you can add to any ordinary week to boost your spirits—breakfast for dinner, movie night, scavenger hunt? Plan what you will do this week here.

_____

_____

_____

162. APPLAUD YOUR EFFORTS. What do you deserve a round of applause for? Go ahead and clap like you want an encore!

_____

_____

_____

163. BREATHE AND FEEL. Close your eyes and focus solely on your breathing for one minute. When you open your eyes, write down a few words that capture how you feel.

164. EXPRESS PHYSICAL NEEDS. Do hugs feed your soul or make you feel super-uncomfortable? Consider how different expressions of love make you feel, then share those feelings with the important people in your life.

_____

_____

_____

_____

165. GET CRAFTY. Clear your mind with an artsy activity—knit or crochet, paint, sketch, whatever you enjoy to bring your focus to this moment. How does it feel?

_____

_____

_____

166. GO TO NEW HEIGHTS. A change of perspective can energize. Where can you get a higher view today?

_____

_____

_____

167. CELEBRATE HAPPY HOUR. What's your favorite hour of the day? What pleasurable elements does it have that you can pull into the rest of your day?

_____

_____

_____

168. SIT AND PREP. When you arrive at a destination, take a moment to sit in your car or stand outside and mentally prepare for whatever comes next. Is there a ritual you can use to mark the transition?

_____

_____

_____

_____

_____

169. TOP IT OFF. Add a special topping to a food or drink you enjoy—from a sprinkle of cinnamon on your coffee to sprinkles on your ice cream or even toast. Sketch the delicacy below.

170. FILL IN PHOTOS. No need to create a whole scrapbook or album in a day! Just grab a few loose photos and fill in some information on their backs. What hidden treasures did you find?

171. MARK THE FOOTHOLDS. What mountain is weighing heavily on your mind this week? Name it below, and mark three milestones along the way where you can rest and see progress.

172. CHOOSE PEACE. Whom can you make peace with today—no matter how much they rattle you—to reclaim your own sense of calm?

_____

_____

_____

173. RELIVE THE DAY. What day would you love to live all over again? Plan a way to make at least parts of it happen.

_____

_____

_____

174. NURTURE YOUR SPIRIT. How can you devote some self-care time to what sparks your spiritual side today?

_____

_____

_____

175. DRESS YOUR FRIDGE. Place fun photos, positive messages, anything that makes you smile front and center on your fridge door. Plan the layout here.

176. WATCH TO LEARN. Add some titles to your TV watch list that can help you develop new skills, live healthier, learn about different cultures, or grow in some other way that's important to you.

_____   _____

_____   _____

_____   _____

177. MAKE IT A BEAUTIFUL DAY. What makes you feel beautiful? Do it, wear it, feel it today.

_____

_____

_____

178. CHOOSE A PERFECT ENDING. How can you end this day feeling wonderful? You're the author!

_____

_____

_____

179. FOCUS ON STRENGTH. Fill the space below with what makes you feel unstoppable.

180. SIT IN THE SUN. Look for the sunbeams and take in their warmth and light. Where did you find them? How did they feel? Cloudy day? Light a candle and bask in its glow.

_____

_____

_____

_____

181. STAY OPEN. Standing in the middle of a doorway, place your forearms on each side of the doorframe. Gently lean forward until you feel a stretch through the front of the chest and shoulders. Hold for 30 seconds. As you extend your upper body, identify what you could be more open to in life.

_____

_____

_____

182. KNOW YOUR TRIGGERS. List your top triggers in the left column, then offer ways to disarm them in the right column.

_____   _____

_____   _____

_____   _____

183. FIND HOPE IN HISTORY. Need inspiration to prevail through tough times? Look back at a moment from history. Where do you sense similarities?

_____

_____

_____

184. REACH THAT GOAL. Visualize yourself reaching a goal or milestone as you draw a symbol of the achievement.

185. PARTNER UP. What is something on your to-do or want-to-accomplish list that would be much easier with a little assistance? Who is the perfect partner?

_____

_____

_____

186. SNOOZE YOUR PHONE. Resist checking your phone immediately after waking up. How does it feel to give yourself a more peaceful entry to the day?

_____

_____

_____

BONUS: Try to wait 30 minutes before checking in with tech.

187. TURN TO A CHILDHOOD COMFORT. What brought you calm in childhood—a certain song or stuffed animal? Bring it back into your life now.

_____

_____

_____

188. DITCH DISCOMFORT. What situation in your life is bringing you discomfort that's not productive in any way? Resolve to walk away.

_____

_____

_____

_____

189. GO TO EXTREMES. Draw your worst character trait to the extreme. Quick temper? Draw yourself as a fire-breathing dragon. Then smile and realize while we all have work to do (every diamond has flaws!), it's not the end of the world.

190. LISTEN TO YOUR BODY. It may feel a little silly at first, but ask your body what it needs. What answer do you get? Follow through.

_____

_____

_____

191. LISTEN TO YOUR GUT. List three times you followed your intuition and something special happened as a result.

1. _____

2. _____

3. _____

192. BE AN ANIMAL. Who are you when you are untamed and feeling free to share the true you? Draw and name your spirit animal below.

BONUS: Add to the scene the keys to feeling free on a daily basis.

193. FEEL THE WEATHER. Describe or draw your current mood as a weather report. Know that it can change as quickly as it came on.

194. SCENT THE SHOWER. Sprinkle a few drops of an essential oil—relaxing or energizing, whichever scent you need—in the corner of your shower. What feelings can you feel lifting away with the aromatic steam?

_____

_____

_____

195. DESIGN YOUR DESKTOP. A cluttered computer screen isn't very inspiring. Plan below the streamlined folders that can organize everything you need on a daily basis. What background matches the vibe you desire?

196. STRENGTHEN YOUR SLEEP. Head to your bed 15 minutes earlier than usual. As you prepare for sleep, say some gentle good-night words to yourself—such as "You did your best today" or "I love who I am, today and tomorrow." Write your good-night message below.

197. CHOOSE TO REFRAME. What happened today that seemed like a catastrophe at the time? Can you see any good in it now that it's in the past?

_____

_____

_____

198. GIVE PARTIAL CREDIT. The best teachers give some credit for doing the work even if you don't arrive at the entirely correct answer. In what situation have you been demanding perfection that you can give yourself partial credit for?

_____

_____

_____

199. GRANT SOME SPACE. Who or what do you need to distance from this week? Give your permission and a plan here.

_____

_____

_____

200. BE PROUD. Give yourself five compliments for the day—from rocking an outfit to handling a difficult situation. Speak to yourself as you would a good friend.

1. _____

2. _____

3. _____

4. _____

5. _____

201. BE YOUR OWN GATEKEEPER. Be mindful of what enters the space of your mind and heart today—from media to mean people. What do you decide to lock out?

_____

_____

_____

202. TARGET RENEWAL. What in your life needs renewal—anything from your passport or a wall color to your creativity and spirit? Promise yourself to seek the newness you need.

_____

_____

_____

_____

203. KNOW YOUR SELF-LOVE LANGUAGE. Just as you find there are ways to show love for friends and family that really resonate, you can identify what self-care modes are most helpful to you. Circle what you appreciate the most.

TANGIBLE GIFTS   PHYSICAL TOUCH

WORDS OF AFFIRMATION

ACTS OF SUPPORT   QUALITY TIME

204. TURN TO YOUR HEART. Place a hand on your heart, feeling the warm touch. As you breathe slowly and deeply, think of a time you felt accepted and loved. Stay in this safe place for at least 30 seconds. Capture the good feelings in words or pictures below.

205. SENSE THE MOMENT. Focus on just this moment—not what happened earlier today or what could possibly be ahead. Use your senses as grounding.

WHAT I SEE: _____ .

WHAT I HEAR: _____ .

WHAT I SMELL: _____ .

WHAT I TOUCH: _____ .

WHAT I TASTE: _____ .

206. REWARD YOURSELF. Set a small goal below to start working toward this week. Draw a star or other symbol on your daily planner or calendar for each day that you do something to support reaching your goal.

_____

_____

_____

_____

207. CONNECT WITH AN ANIMAL. Hang out with a pet (yours or a friend's) or watch an animal video or show. What can you take away from these masters of self-care?

_____

_____

_____

_____

208. CHECK IN. Take a moment to simply write about how you're feeling right now.

_____

_____

_____

_____

209. WAKE UP YOUR SHOWER. Try starting your shower at a comfortably warm temperature, then slowly cool down the water at the very end. According to research, short bouts of mild cold exposure seem to help the brain work better. How did it feel?

_____

_____

_____

210. SPRITZ YOUR PILLOW. Before bed, spray your pillow with a calming scent—an essential oil blend or fabric refresher. As you spray, make a wish for tomorrow and record it.

_____

_____

_____

_____

211. SORT THE CRITICISM. What words of criticism have you been dealt lately? While trying not to take any of them as personal attacks, sort the criticisms into the categories below.

SOMETHING TO LEARN

SOMETHING TO LET GO

_____   _____

_____   _____

_____   _____

_____   _____

212. PUT DOWN THE GUILT.
Think of something you've been feeling guilty about. Then pick up an object of decent weight in your surroundings and hold it for 10 to 20 seconds. As you carefully set the object down, release the burden on your mind too. What did you let go?

213. FREE YOUR FLOW. Recall a day that was super-productive—whether you organized at home or finished off a project at work or school. What factors helped keep you focused and not overwhelmed?

_____

_____

_____

214. READ TO INSPIRE. Whose life can you learn from? Find a biography that connects with you. What will you read?

_____

_____

_____

_____

BONUS: Come back and record words of inspiration here or highlight them as you read.

215. ENCOURAGE A SPARK. What's something in your community that gets you excited—recycling, outdoor recreation, libraries? Follow a web page or social account with updates in that area. Where can you pitch in?

_____

_____

_____

_____

216. FOCUS ON FOOD. Write down everything you ate and drank today and how you felt afterward. Do any patterns emerge?

<u>FOOD/DRINK</u>   <u>HOW I FELT</u>

_____   _____

_____   _____

_____   _____

_____   _____

_____   _____

_____   _____

_____   _____

217. TAKE A STEP. Set one fitness goal. (It could be anything from feeling less stiff and tired to running a marathon.) Then promise yourself one step you can take toward that goal this week.

MY GOAL: _____

_____

MY PROMISE: _____

_____

218. CLEAR THE CLUTTER. What little space can you tackle to bring more calm to your environment and your mind?

_____

_____

_____

219. STRENGTHEN THE CONNECTION. How would you describe your relationship with yourself? How could it better?

_____

_____

_____

220. LET IT GO. What are you physically holding on to that it's time to release— an unfinished project that haunts you, a gift that's more clutter than cherished, something from your past that no longer fits you? Put it in the trash, recycling, or donate pile right now.

_____

_____

_____

_____

221. SET BOUNDARIES. In what area of your life do you need to set better boundaries? Make a resolution by writing it below and drawing a fence around the word(s). Then make choices that support your goal.

222. FEEL SAFE. Cover the space below with all the things that make you feel safe—physically and emotionally. Then imagine them surrounding you.

223. LEND A LITTLE EXPERTISE. Who in your life would welcome help or motivation that you are qualified to give? Reach out today.

_____

_____

_____

_____

_____

224. DESIGN A MESSAGE. Write a positive mantra in fancy lettering below, take a picture of it, and set it as the wallpaper on your computer screen.

225. GO AHEAD, CRY. When was the last time you had a good cry? Could you use one now? Give yourself permission.

_____

_____

_____

226. CHOOSE YOUR MOVE. Move your body any way you enjoy for one minute. How does it feel? Do you keep moving even longer?

_____

_____

_____

227. SET A PACE. The best runners reach the finish line and feel strong along the way with smart pacing. In what parts of your life could you push your effort? In what parts of your life do you need to ease up?

PUSH	RELAX
_____	_____
_____	_____
_____	_____
_____	_____

228. MANIFEST IT. Close your eyes and envision how you want the rest of this week to go. Sketch the best parts below, and get ready to make them happen.

229. LOOK INTO ALTERNATIVES. Plot out an alternative therapy—such as acupuncture, hydrotherapy, or Ayurveda—that you are open to trying for self-care. Make a list of questions you have.

_____

_____

_____

_____

_____

230. FEEL YOUR FIERCENESS. List all the ways in which you are strong.

_____ _____

_____ _____

_____ _____

_____ _____

231. SALUTE THE TRUE YOU. When you feel most like yourself, what are you doing?

_____

_____

_____

232. CLAIM SELF-CARE MINUTES. Wake up just a bit earlier tomorrow morning. How will you enjoy the extra time to ease into your day?

_____

_____

_____

_____

233. SPICE IT UP. Choose five new herbs or blends to add to your collection. Let flavor, health benefits, or adventure direct your selections.

1. _____

2. _____

3. _____

4. _____

5. _____

234. FEEL PART OF THE CYCLE. Look for a way to show nature a little TLC. You could pick up litter, start to compost, or set up a bird feeder. What do you choose, and how does it make you feel?

_____

_____

_____

_____

_____

235. NOTICE THE DETAILS. Whether you're walking through an art museum or your own backyard, focus on the details of what you're viewing. What do you see when you take a closer look? Does it help you get out of your own head for a while?

_____

_____

_____

236. CLAIM YOUR SPACE. Where can you go in your home to indulge in a little self-care time? Is there anything that space needs to make it even more inviting?

_____

_____

_____

237. TREAT YOUR MIND TO MEDITATION. Whatever focus you need, you can find a directed meditation through apps or online guides. Record how you feel before and after the meditation exercise.

BEFORE: _____

_____

AFTER: _____

_____

238. SEEK GOOD NEWS. Find a positive story in the news today. What did you find, and how does it make you feel?

_____

_____

_____

_____

239. SHARE THE KINDNESS. What is one of your favorite ways to show kindness to others? How can you turn it around and share that kindness with yourself?

_____

_____

_____

240. RUB IN THE LOVE. Take a minute before bed to rub on body lotion. As you do, think or speak out loud positive statements about your body and how it blesses you. Write the statements below as a reminder.

_____

_____

_____

241. WRITE YOURSELF A PEP TALK. What do you need to hear in the locker room of life? Believe!

_____

_____

_____

_____

242. CURATE A COLLECTION. Curate a collection on Instagram or save to a folder on Facebook to create a gathering of something you love. Anti-social? Create a folder on your desktop. What will you collect to turn to when you need a smile—dog photos, inspirational quotes, soothing home designs?

_____

_____

_____

243. SEE THE PROGRESS. Fill in the blanks below to remind yourself you are moving forward even if you haven't reached your destination.

I am _____ ing.

I am _____ ing.

I am _____ ing.

I am _____ ing.

I am _____ ing.

244. GREET THAT FEELING. What emotion is leading the way today? Without judging, simply name it below. Recognizing it is the first step to either amplifying its energy or showing it the door.

245. PUZZLE IT OUT. Choose a word search, crossword, sudoku, find-the-difference, or any kind of puzzle book that you can carry on the go. How does working through a few clues make you feel?

_____

_____

_____

246. BE YOUR OWN FRIEND. What was challenging or felt like a failure today? Speak to yourself with the words you would offer a good friend.

_____

_____

_____

247. LET IT BURN. Toss or burn something that symbolizes what you don't want in your life. What do you choose, and how does it feel?

_____

_____

_____

_____

248. OCCUPY YOUR ANXIETY. Grab something that can keep your hands busy and distract you. It could be a fidget spinner, a silky ribbon, anything that moves you out of your head and into a pleasant tactile place. What can you use at home, and what can you use on the go?

249. LEARN NEW WORDS. Choose a new language to begin to learn, or aim to expand your own first language's vocabulary. What words do you discover?

_____

_____

_____

250. SPRITZ IT ON. Sample essential oils at a local store. Which scent stands out, and where can you use it to bring a certain quality to your day—clearheadedness in the car, energy for a walk or run, calm at bedtime?

_____

_____

_____

251. LIVE THE DAYDREAM. Give yourself permission to simply imagine a dream day. Note what you see, hear, taste, smell, and touch.

_____

_____

_____

252. MAKE A WISH ON A STAR. After taking in the night sky, draw a star here and write your wish inside.

253. ACCEPT ADVICE. Who gives you the best advice? What do they have to say to you right now?

_____

_____

_____

254. START OVER. Where in your life are you ready for a fresh start? Write the words in pencil, then erase them to remind yourself that you can always start over.

255. BRING VACATION VIBES. How can you inject a little bit of vacation into an ordinary day?

_____

_____

_____

256. WEAR IT WELL. Wear something bold or uniquely you today. Record any compliments.

_____

_____

_____

_____

BONUS: Include a photo of yourself wearing your choice fabulously.

257. PARK YOUR WORRIES. Whatever worries are speeding through your mind's superhighway, park them in the spaces below.

258. BREATHE THE CHANGE. Take deep, cleansing breaths for a full minute. Record how you feel before and then after.

_____

_____

_____

BONUS: Measure your heart rate and blood pressure before and after deep breathing.

259. MAKE THE GRADE. What grade would you give yourself for attention to self-care today? If it's not as high as you would like, what can you do right now for some extra credit?

_____

_____

_____

_____

260. DO THE TWIST. Take the last negative thing you said or thought to yourself and give it a positive twist.

_____

_____

_____

261. CONNECT WITH NATURE. Whether you splash in a puddle or walk barefoot on grass, find a way to make a physical connection with an element in nature. How do you feel after the contact?

_____

_____

_____

262. BE YOUR OWN FAN. Draw a sign cheering yourself on. Include a foam finger if you feel so moved.

GO!

263. FOCUS ON GRATITUDE. Fill the space below with what you are grateful for today.

264. PICK A PODCAST. Even if you're already a podcast fan, try venturing outside of your usual circle of listening this week. Set a time when you will appreciate it the most.

_____

_____

_____

_____

265. INDULGE YOUR PASSION. What are five topics (fun or serious) that you love to discuss? Set up a time to talk with someone who is just as passionate about at least one of them.

1. _____

2. _____

3. _____

4. _____

5. _____

266. EXPLORE A CULTURE. Try a new type of food or music. What did you appreciate about the experience?

_____

_____

_____

267. APPRECIATE DISCOVERIES. What truths (little or big) have you discovered about yourself or the world this week?

_____

_____

_____

268. SIT IN SILENCE. Imagine all the noise in your life right now just drifting away as you note the sources of drama on the lines below.

_____ _____

_____

_____ _____

_____

269. START A GIF EXCHANGE. Agree with a friend to send cute GIFs through text or to flood each other's social media with adorable images that will make you smile at least once a week. Who's your partner, and what kind of images do you want to see?

_____

_____

_____

_____

270. EXAMINE APOLOGIES. When was the last time you said "I'm sorry" when you didn't do anything wrong ("I'm sorry, but this isn't what I ordered") or were taking responsibility for someone else ("I'm sorry—he's not usually like this")? Write out the apology below, then cross out "I'm sorry."

_____

_____

_____

271. EXTEND YOUR DEADLINE. What decision are you feeling rushed to make? Give yourself more time with a reasonable deadline.

_____

_____

_____

272. TURN UP LAUGHTER. Watch your favorite comedy show. How does it connect with you?

_____

_____

_____

273. LET IN THE LIGHT. List five places in your home and on the go where you can find great natural light. Spend time in as many as you can this week.

1. _____

2. _____

3. _____

4. _____

5. _____

274. FUEL CREATIVITY. Where can you go this week to instantly surround yourself with innovation and inspiration—maybe an art exhibit (in person or online) or a craft supply store? Post a pic or describe it below.

275. SAY YES TO YOGA. Sink into Child's Pose. How do you feel in the pose and when you emerge from it?

_____

_____

_____

276. WALK AROUND THE CORNER. What's something you see in your neighborhood that you've never seen before? How does it encourage you to have fresh eyes everywhere you go?

_____

_____

_____

277. TAKE THE CAKE. Saving cakes for only birthdays and weddings is boring. What simple event or milestone can you celebrate with a cake this week? What flavor will you order or make?

_____

_____

_____

_____

278. CHALK A MESSAGE. Where can you share a positive message with someone else or yourself? Plan your chalk drawing here.

279. BREAK THE RULE. Eat dessert before (or as!) dinner. Stay up past your usual bedtime—as long as you're doing something memorable. What little "rule" would it feel good to break today?

_____

_____

_____

280. CLEAR THE PAPER TRAIL. Make a list of the biggest sources of paper clutter in your home. Are there ways you can declutter by signing up for online banking, receipts, health-test results, coupons, and anything else on your offender list?

_____   _____

_____   _____

_____   _____

281. FEEL THE LOVE. Describe a time you felt truly loved and understood.

_____

_____

_____

_____

282. SAY NO. Be ready to say no to something today that feels like an unnecessary burden. Color in the word *no* as your intention below.

283. CLOSE THAT CHAPTER. When were you robbed of a proper goodbye? Say what you would have wanted to say here.

_____

_____

_____

_____

284. FOLD FOR FUN. Search online for "one-minute origami." Getting crafty will occupy your thoughts with creativity and possibility. Share what you make in words or pictures.

BONUS: Give your creation to a friend.

285. PLAN FOR AN EVENT. What upcoming event are you looking forward to? Plan what you want to wear, what you need to bring, how you expect the day to go. Anticipation can be a powerful, positive emotion.

_____

_____

_____

_____

286. KNOW YOUR INFLUENCERS. Who is a good influence on you? Set a time to connect this week.

_____

_____

_____

287. PICK OUT A GREETING CARD. You'll find humor and positive thoughts, even if you don't even have an occasion in mind. What words did you read that connected with you?

_____

_____

_____

288. FEED YOUR HEALTH. Find and post two new healthy recipes to try in the next week. Coming up with new culinary ideas is also a great way to get your creative juices flowing.

289. MAKE A PROMISE TO YOURSELF. Whatever it is, no matter how big or small, keep it!

_____

_____

_____

290. LOOK IN THE MIRROR. List as many positive attributes—outer or inner—as you can see or sense.

_____

_____

_____

_____

291. TURN YOUR HANGERS. Make your clothes hangers hook from the back. After you wear something that feels great, flip it the other way to mark a keeper. Remove any pieces that don't feel like you. What's the first keeper? What's the first item for the donation pile?

_____

_____

_____

_____

292. REBOOT AND REFRESH. Restart your phone, computer, and smartwatch at least once this week. While your devices back up data and look for upgrades, how can you enjoy a tech time-out?

_____

_____

_____

_____

293. HIGHLIGHT SKILLS AND GOALS. If you're on a professional social network, consider how changing just a few keywords might open new opportunities or help your current colleagues see your value in a new light. Not currently on a network? Join! What skills and goals are important to you to include?

_____

_____

_____

_____

294. SCHEDULE A FITTING. Want the best fit for a suit, sneakers, or a bra? Go to a pro. How does the fit feel with some professional input and measures?

_____

_____

_____

_____

295. RELAX YOUR MUSCLES. Lie down and close your eyes. As you inhale, tense one body part and hold. As you exhale, say a cue word like _melt_ and release the tension, letting that part relax into your supporting surface. Work through as many tense spots as you can in the time you have. What cue word did you choose? Where did you feel the most tension released?

_____

_____

_____

_____

296. SET 60 SECONDS ON THE CLOCK. What's the hardest thing on your to-do list today—exercising, paying bills, starting a work project? Note it below, then set a timer and do it for a minute. After 60 seconds, you'll find it easier to keep going.

_____

_____

_____

_____

_____

297. STOP IN AT YOUR LOCAL LIBRARY. Do you borrow a book, pick up donated seeds to plant, or simply browse the bulletin boards for upcoming events?

_____

_____

_____

_____

_____

298. LEAVE WORRIES AT THE DOOR. What little ritual—like removing your shoes—can you do when you come home to signal that it's time to leave any burdens of the day behind?

_____

_____

_____

_____

299. POST NOTES. Jot down a few positive messages or helpful reminders on sticky notes. Spread them where you will see them throughout the day. How did it feel to find them?

300. CREATE A WORD CLOUD.

Search for a word cloud generator, then enter words with positivity or special meaning. Plan your focus words here.

301. MAKE A DONATION. Giving is a great feeling. What charity do you choose?

_____

_____

_____

302. FACE A FEAR. Anxious about public speaking? Sign up for a workshop. Afraid of heights? Locate a zip-lining course. What fear are you ready to face, and what's your next step?

_____

_____

_____

303. FEEL ALL THE FEELS. What emotions do you tend to label "bad" and push deep down? How could you let them out healthfully?

_____

_____

_____

304. PULL OUT AN AWARD. Find an award or honor you've received—even a really complimentary letter or email. How does it make you feel to revisit it? Does it inspire any new goals?

_____

_____

_____

_____

305. HAVE A HAPPY HOLIDAY. What's the next holiday on the calendar
that you will celebrate? Make a list of what you want to include and
what you want to skip for a truly happy, stress-free celebration.

HOLIDAY	DO THIS	SKIP THIS
_____	_____	_____
_____	_____	_____
_____	_____	_____
_____	_____	_____

306. MAKE A TURN. In what areas of your life are you at turning points, where you
could choose a different, better-for-you path?

_____

_____

_____

307. COLOR YOUR MOOD. What color would you name your mood today?
What circumstances or people in your life could be coloring that view?

_____

_____

_____

308. NAME NAMES. List all of the affectionate names friends and family call you. Mark a heart next to your favorite.

309. APPRECIATE TOUCH. What are your favorite ways to connect physically with close contacts—hugs, hand holding, encouraging shoulder rubs? Where can you find what you need today?

_____

_____

_____

_____

310. HEAR THE INSPIRATION. What sound—from rolling ocean waves to a loved one's encouraging words—brings you comfort and courage? How can you carry it with you everywhere you go?

_____

_____

_____

_____

311. OPEN UP LIGHT. How can you add more light to the indoor spaces in which you spend the most time?

_____

_____

_____

_____

312. WATCH FOR THE WOWS. What made you think or say "wow" today?

_____

_____

_____

_____

313. MAKE A FRESH START. What worries are you holding on to from the past week? Release them here.

_____

_____

_____

_____

314. REMEMBER A GIFT. What's the best gift you ever received? What did it show about how much the giver knows you and values the relationship?

_____

_____

_____

_____

315. THANK YOURSELF FOR CARING. What is one way you have cared for yourself today? Write a thank-you note to you.

_____

_____

_____

_____

316. CHOOSE FOR YOU. What popular healthy habit just doesn't work for you? Give yourself permission to let it go if it's truly not working.

_____

_____

_____

_____

317. INK THE CALENDAR. What are three events in the next few months you can put on the calendar now and look forward to?

1. _____

2. _____

3. _____

318. KNOW YOUR CONTROL. Make a list of the thoughts weighing on you right now. Then go back and cross out the ones over which you honestly have no, or very little, control.

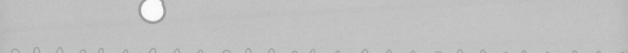

319. MOVE THE NEEDLE. Note the areas of your life that are improving—not perfect, but moving in the right direction.

_____

_____

_____

320. FIND CALM IN WORDS. Make a list of ten words or phrases that bring you peace.

1. _____
2. _____
3. _____
4. _____
5. _____

6. _____
7. _____
8. _____
9. _____
10. _____

BONUS: Choose one to place somewhere in your day—maybe on a mug or bracelet.

321. FIND HUMOR IN WORDS. Make a list of ten words or phrases that make you laugh.

1. _____
2. _____
3. _____
4. _____
5. _____

6. _____
7. _____
8. _____
9. _____
10. _____

322. SAVE ENERGY. What people and situations are energy drains in your life? How can you choose to spend time with people and situations that recharge you instead?

_____

_____

_____

_____

323. BLOW TO LOWER PRESSURE. As you make a thumbs-up, blow on your thumb. This little trick stimulates the vagus nerve, which tells your body to lower your blood pressure and decrease your heart rate. What part of the day did you just blow off?

_____

_____

_____

_____

324. TAKE IT SLOW. What are three things you would benefit from slowing down today?

1. _____

2. _____

3. _____

325. GO YOUR OWN WAY. What unique thoughts and paths are you proud of in your life right now?

_____

_____

_____

326. SEE THE WIN. What past personal victory can you visualize when you need to feel more confident? Sketch or describe it below.

327. ASK THE QUESTIONS. Whether it's why someone in your life is acting a certain way or what professional step you should take next, jot down the questions filling your head so you can find a little space.

_____

_____

_____

_____

328. UNSUBSCRIBE. Save your in-box from overwhelm and yourself from distraction by taking a second to click on those unsubscribe links. Be ruthless with anything you don't truly benefit from. How many goodbyes do you make? How does it feel?

_____

_____

_____

_____

329. KEEP THE BEST. Sort through your beauty and personal care products. What can you ditch that doesn't work for you—in terms of results or time? It will be easier and quicker to find your faves when they have space to shine.

_____

_____

_____

_____

330. SAY IT OUT LOUD. Look at yourself in the mirror and say whatever strengthening words your heart needs to hear. Then write them here as a reminder.

331. END THE WAIT. What have you been waiting for the perfect timing or conditions to do? What first step can you take right now?

_____

_____

_____

332. FLUSH IT. Whenever you flush a toilet today or throw something in the trash, think about what else you can clear out of your life. List a few of your realizations here.

_____

_____

_____

333. SURROUND YOURSELF WITH BEAUTY. Fill your spaces and day with whatever you find beautiful—from music and art to people and nature. What do you include?

_____

_____

_____

_____

334. AWARD YOURSELF. Acknowledge your recent efforts or achievements—silly or serious—by designing your own trophy, medal, or certificate below.

335. ADMIT YOUR HURTS. What's hurting you emotionally or physically? Recognizing the pain is the first step toward healing.

_____

_____

_____

336. START A PUZZLE. Connecting even just a piece each day can help you feel more confident in your ability to focus and find solutions. What beyond-the-puzzle solution are you seeking?

_____

_____

_____

337. GET YOUR HANDS DIRTY. It can be so freeing to dig into something physically with your hands. Maybe it's dirt, clay, finger paints, or bread dough. What do you choose and how does it feel?

_____

_____

_____

_____

_____

338. SEE POSSIBILITY IN EVERY CHOICE. What was the best choice you made today—whether it was a simple food decision that brought you pleasure or a life-changing fork in the road?

_____

_____

_____

_____

339. CELEBRATE YOUR BODY. Cover this space with what you consider the most amazing things your body has allowed you to do so far in your life.

340. ELEVATE SMALL VICTORIES. What went well for you today—from the coffee brewing just as you like it to putting a decent dent in a long-term project? Cover the space below with all the good.

341. PUT DOWN THE PHONE. When you find yourself waiting today, choose something to do other than scrolling—maybe strike up a conversation or read a few pages of a book. What do you do, and how does it feel?

_____

_____

_____

_____

_____

342. BREATHE IN THE AIR. Where is the air that you love to breathe—by the sea, at the coffee shop, in the garden, in the kitchen of a great listener who makes the best cookies, or somewhere else? When can you go there?

_____

_____

_____

_____

_____

343. FIND A SURPRISE. How did you surprise yourself or someone else in a pleasant way today? No surprises? Plan one for a special person tomorrow.

_____

_____

_____

344. WRITE YOUR EPITAPH. How do you want to be remembered? Are you living your life aligned with your priorities?

_____

_____

_____

345. CONSIDER YOURSELF AN EXPLORER. Where can you roam or head in a new direction today?

_____

_____

_____

_____

346. FREE THAT SCREAM. What are you screaming inside? Write it below in bold letters, then release it in a safe physical space, like your car, into a pillow, or on an empty beach.

347. SIMPLY SCRIBBLE. No one is immune to frustration. As you think of a situation that's driving you insane, scribble in the space below to work out those feelings.

348. SCAN THE HORIZON. What's just getting started in your life that you're excited to see develop?

_____

_____

_____

_____

349. ALLOW TRANSITIONS. The craziest parts of our days can be rushing from one task to another. Look at your schedule for today or tomorrow. What calming transitions can you build in—for example, a cup of tea or just quiet time between appointments?

_____

_____

_____

_____

_____

350. EMBRACE YOUR FLAWS. Accepting yourself includes accepting shortcomings. Jot down some of your flaws. Next to each, write "It's OK" or "I'm working on it."

_____   _____

_____   _____

_____   _____

_____   _____

351. CLEAR A PATH. What daily distractions or temptations can you remove?

_____

_____

_____

352. WORK YOUR MAGIC. Make a list of things that come easily to you.

_____   _____

_____   _____

_____   _____

_____   _____

BONUS: Identify something from the list above that could help someone else this week.

353. FEEL THE CLEANSE. Pop in a load of laundry and watch as the water and soap begin to go to work. What can you envision cleansing from your life?

_____

_____

_____

_____

354. FUND A GOAL. Set a financial goal below—whether to clear away debt or save for a big purchase. Then open a separate bank account where you can stash funds toward your goal.

_____

_____

_____

_____

_____

355. ORDER IN. What special dish will make it a special day?

_____

_____

_____

356. LOOK FOR LUCK. Carry a good luck charm with you wherever you go today. Not superstitious? It can be simply a photo of friends or family to remind you that you are lucky to be loved. What physical object makes you feel lucky?

_____

_____

_____

357. FACE THE SHOULDS. What are the most frequent "you should . . ." statements you hear from other people? List them below, then cross out the shoulds that aren't aligned with your best interests or goals for yourself.

_____   _____

_____   _____

_____   _____

_____   _____

358. BE BOTH. Draw an image below of something beautiful and strong—a sunflower in a rainstorm, a steel bridge reaching into the sky, a superhero with a flowing cape. Envision yourself with this duality.

359. HAVE "NO" OPTIONS. *No* is always a strong word that helps you set boundaries. But in case you'd like more choices, brainstorm a few words or phrases you can use to draw the line clearly and without wavering. Examples: "I don't have time in my schedule." "That doesn't work for me."

_____   _____

_____   _____

_____   _____

_____   _____

_____   _____

○──○──○──○──○──○──○──○──○──○

360. TELL YOURSELF NO. In what situations or thoughts do you need to tell yourself no? Where is tough love needed in your life to protect self-care?

_____

_____

_____

_____

_____

361. TAKE PRIDE IN YOUR VOICE. Find a way to lift your voice today in a place where you may have shied away in the past. Share that idea in a brainstorm meeting. Stand up for a target of gossip. Serenade a loved one with no trace of self-consciousness. Where does your voice ring out?

_____

_____

_____

362. CREATE A CIRCLE OF CARE. In the circles below, write the names of the people whose care you feel is your responsibility.

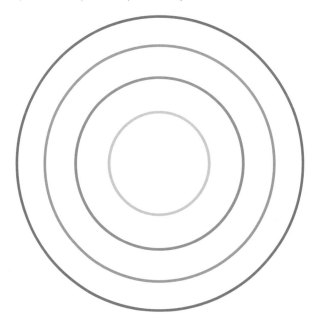

363. CENTER YOURSELF.
Go back to the last prompt on the previous page. Who is in the center circle? If it's you, applaud yourself. If it's not, rework the focus here to include yourself in the center.

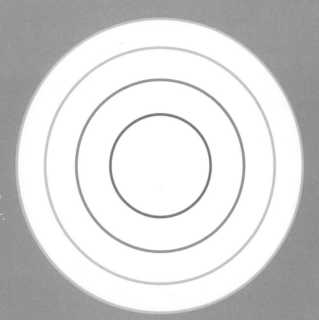

364. FOCUS ON THE GOOD. Fill the space below with what made you smile today.

365. CONTINUE TO TAKE A MINUTE TO CHECK IN. Each day, ask yourself, how was I kind to . . .

. . . MY MIND?

_____

_____

_____

. . . MY BODY?

_____

_____

_____

. . . MY SOUL?

_____

_____

_____